Start Figs  Beginners Guide On How To Grow Fig Trees (*Ficus carica*)

By Gaia Min

Table Of Contents

Table Of Contents	2
What Are Fig Trees	4
Importance Of Fig Trees Throughout History	7
Where Can Common Figs Grow	11
Best Soil For Fig Trees	14
How To Plant A Fig Tree	18
Should You Grow Figs In Containers	23
Pros and Cons of Container Growing Figs	24
Pros	24
Cons	25
Ways To Keep Ants and Pests Off Of Your Figs	29
How and When To Prune A Fig Tree	34
Open Center Pruning	36
Rejuvenation Pruning	37
Pinching Figs During Growing Season	38
How To Take Fig Cuttings (get free plants)	40
Breba Crop vs Main Crop	44
Are There Wasps Inside Of Figs?	47

Open-Eye vs Closed-Eye Figs	50
How To Winterize Your Fig Tree	**53**
List Of Common Fig Varieties	**58**
Popular Varieties	59

What Are Fig Trees

Fig trees refer to a genus of plants known as *Ficus*. The common fig tree, known as *Ficus carica,* is the main focus of this book. As the name implies, *Ficus Carica* is the fig species responsible for the most widely consumed fruit that people are familiar with.

Common figs are relatively small trees, normally growing only 10-30 feet. Native to the Middle East, they have a rather distinctive appearance compared to most other trees. With large, lobed palmate leaves (shaped like a hand) and smooth bark it's not hard to basically identify these plants even when they have no fruit on them. They have growth with multiple stems originating from the base but can be trained into single-stem trees with proper pruning.

The fruit of the common fig is very soft and perishes extremely fast. Depending on the variety it can range from slightly sweet to sickly sweet like honey. While the fruit decays rapidly once ripe, figs don't ripen all their fruit at once, allowing for multiple harvests. This is both a positive and negative since that means you will likely need multiple trees if you want large harvests throughout the season.

Another distinctive trait about figs is the latex contained in nearly all portions of the plant. Though some may refer to the latex for possible remedies, it is best to take caution. The latex is a mild irritant and can cause serious allergic reactions in susceptible individuals. You can notice the latex by the milky white sap exuded by the plant when damaged. Fig trees rely on their caustic sap to protect themselves and unripe fruit from predators and diseases.

The sap can cause chemical burns on sensitive skin.

As a result, it is often advised to handle fig trees wearing a pair of gloves and avoid eating unripe fruit. Wash hands thoroughly after handling fig material and keep it away from young children who may place it in their mouths.

Fig sap is more damaging if the contaminated skin is exposed to sunlight. A condition known as photodermatitis can occur under extreme circumstances. Cases of photodermatitis caused by fig trees were documented in children who used crushed leaves while playing outside. As with any plant, if you are new to fig trees, always use caution. The chemicals in plants vary and allergic reactions are always possible, though rare.

Importance Of Fig Trees Throughout History

Despite my previous warnings, it's also important to note that humans have had a very close relationship with the *Ficus* genus. The plants have been seen as essential to human survival and evolution in hot regions. The historical genus is significantly referenced in several religions and is still used as a staple resource for certain groups of people.

A large part of fig's critical role can be attributed to its hardiness and ability to spread. They can establish in drier conditions compared to other fruit trees and create an understory that helps build an environment for smaller plants to grow. The food generated by figs also supports a significant amount of wildlife. Plants like figs are referred to as "pioneer" species that allow an entire ecosystem to develop due to its establishment.

The common fig, *Ficus carica*, is not truly representative of a fig's grand structure. The Banyan tree, *Ficus benghalensis,* is a display of fig's true magnificence. This species of trees has one of the largest canopy spreads of any tree in the world due to its unique growing habit. Aerial roots extend from the canopy and grow down into the soil, allowing it to continue spreading for centuries.

The forest generative nature of figs and their reliable growth made them important, both ecologically and economically for locals. Farmers used the fallen leaves and sprouts as supplemental animal feed, sellers used the bark for clothing and crafts, and warriors even relied on the wood for making shields. People even found ways to prepare medicines from leaves, bark, and sap. The many uses of figs and how enabling they were for societies resulted in them gaining religious and spiritual significance.

Some believe the fig to be the recurring "Tree of Life" seen in many religions, though there are other trees also suspected of this.

Today, figs are no less important. The genus still makes up a large part of tropical forests and supports a wide range of biodiversity. Economically, fig use is expected to keep increasing with over 1 ton of fruit produced annually at the industrial level. In addition, *Ficus* is one of the most common genera of houseplants in the world. They help bring a bit of nature indoors, improving the air quality and boosting moods. The common fig is also gaining more popularity with a very devout number of collectors.

The future of figs is still left to be seen. With climate change reducing the amount of fruit set in some species and decline in their pollinator, sexual propagation among figs may grow stagnant. With no new offspring or fruit, ecosystems dependent on the fig tree may be disrupted and eventually collapse. However, humans can always interfere (in a good way) to stop that from happening. The future of figs will certainly be worth keeping an eye on in the coming years as the species is too important to let crumple. Who knows, maybe someone reading this will be inspired to study fig trees as a career. If so, don't forget to give me a shoutout!

Where Can Common Figs Grow

Figs don't hesitate to grow if given a suitable spot but finding that suitable spot is crucial. Odds are, you will need to worry about your area being too cold rather than too hot. Common figs are actually one of the more cold hardy of fig species but even they don't like temperatures to drop too low. You will find that they often die down to the roots below zone 7, but grow back once temperatures warm up. Currently, there is a cold tolerant fig ideal for zones lower than 7, named the Chicago Hardy Fig. Zone 5 is the farthest you can expect to grow figs. Beyond that and the season will probably be too short for fruit to ripen even if it survives the cold.

Figs need full sun for best fruiting, though they will tolerate light shade. A spot that receives sunlight late into the evening can help against nighttime lows if it is near a structure that can radiate the heat back. Otherwise, you will want to place your tree where it will not get sunlight in the early morning or late afternoon during Winter. Without a structure to radiant the heat back during the night, the temperature swings will do more harm than good.

Winter winds is another issue you need to consider before choosing where to grow a fig. If the plant is left exposed during Winter, it greatly increases the chance of top growth damage. This injury is known as Winter desiccation. Plants can't take up water faster than it is being lost when dormant. Winds during warm months are less of an issue because relative humidity is often high, minimizing water loss.

To protect from the Winter wind, you need to find out the direction of prevailing winds for your location. This information can usually be found online. If not, contacting a local weather official can also help in obtaining this info. If you already have a space planned for your fig tree, find out its relation to the prevailing winds and consider building a protective buffer or planting a screen of plants.

You will also need to consider the root zone of fig trees before planting. Figs have very aggressive roots that can extend several meters away from the plant. While common figs aren't the most destructive, they still spread vigorously. Testament to this, I've had fig cuttings fill 5 gallon pots with thick roots in one growing season. Caution should be taken when planting a fig near any structure of underground piping. This often leads to people preferring to grow figs in containers, rather than in the ground.

Lastly, the soil is the final determination of where you can plant a fig. Due to its complexity, I will give soil its own dedicated section for discussion.

Best Soil For Fig Trees

Soil for fig trees deserves its own topic because soil is often more complex than temperature or plant growth habits. While a plant often has soil it finds favorably, it often isn't strict or impossible to grow in something different. In addition, it's possible to amend soil to make it more optimal for fig growing.

The first thing to recognize is that the goal of growing fig trees is to produce fruit. Sounds obvious but you won't believe how many people become focused on leaf growth rather than fruit production. Healthy leaves are not indicative of quality fruit production. High fertility in soil can make for a nice looking plant but low yields. That is because some elements for leafy plant growth interfere with elements needed for fruit production when present in too high of quantities. So don't think you can plant a fig and just pour fertilizer irresponsibly to acquire the desired outcome.

Figs typically like a neutral to slightly acidic pH around 6.5-7.0. Some varieties may like it more acidic than others. While most ornamental gardeners rarely concern themselves with pH values, it is critical for fruit trees. One of the properties of soil pH is that it controls what nutrients a plant can take up from the soil. You could have very good soil, nutrient-wise, but still see nutrient deficiencies in plants because of pH issues. This is commonly seen with inexperienced tomato gardeners who supplement with sources of calcium to correct blossom-end rot. They often add the amendment without even doing a soil test. When the amendment fails to address the issue then they realize it may be a pH problem but now have more issues depending on how much calcium they added.

It's always best to do a soil test and amend the site BEFORE planting in it.

Fixing pH and making mineral amendments is much easier if done before the time of planting.

Preferably the season before. Changes in soil pH can take 1-2 years depending on the substance being added. Choosing what to add for calcium is also important as it can affect your pH. Limestone can add calcium and will increase pH making it better on acidic soil. Gypsum also adds calcium but has neutral pH making it better for already balanced soil. Remember, you don't want your soil too far in either direction of the pH scale.

In addition to nutrient composition, the soil structure should be close to a loam or sandy loam but figs aren't too picky. Rather than exact composition, they like to have a lot of organic matter present with good drainage. Adding a top dressing of compost and mulch is also very beneficial. However, it's important to remember that you don't want your site to be too much richer than the surrounding soil. That may encourage the fig to treat its planting soil like a pot rather than spread its roots outward. **Never remove the original soil to fill with purchased planting mix when planting in the ground.**

Speaking of planting mix, you may be looking to grow figs in a container. While the information above is still relevant, you will find that potted plants will need more fertilization than those grown in the ground. Without the ability to spread, roots are limited to the nutrients in the pot which can get washed out over time. In-ground figs rarely need fertilizer, but potted ones do. Personally, I mix a slow release organic fertilizer into the potting soil and also add used coffee grounds as a top dressing. However, after one season it will become necessary to either repot the tree with more fertile soil or start using an organic soluble fertilizer, high in phosphorus and potassium but low in nitrogen.

How To Plant A Fig Tree

Planting a fig isn't too complicated once you have found the proper location and analyzed the soil. Though you can plant a tree any time of the year, it is best to do so early spring or early fall. Like most trees, you want to dig a hole twice the width of the root ball and plant at a depth that leaves the roots leveled with the soil. I highly recommend adding a 3" layer of mulch to the new plant site, but be sure not to put mulch against the base of the plant. Mulch at the base promotes disease and pests. In addition, I've found that figs are much less likely to send up new shoots from the base if it is covered with mulch.

One problem that is prevalent with transplanting figs is their willingness to entangle roots. Before planting, you will likely need to untangle your fig's root ball and even prune it by a third or even half in extreme cases. If roots aren't fixed at the time of planting they will compromise plant growth and possibly lead to an early death for the plant as it essentially strangles itself.

New gardeners are often very hesitant to cut roots but I can assure you that the plant almost always benefits from it. Figs, in particular, recover very fast from root pruning.

If you want to go the extra mile when transplanting, here are some additional steps that can be taken but aren't entirely necessary.

- The day before transplanting, water your plant thoroughly and try to transplant first thing in the morning. This will reduce transplant shock, especially if you have to do a heavy root pruning.

- Consider soaking the roots of the transplant in rooting hormone or water infused with willow stems. This can stimulate root growth early and help the plant establish faster.

- Inoculate your fig tree's roots with a mycorrhizae supplement, usually available as a powder. Although mycorrhizae occur in nature, they can be void in potting mixes the fig tree has grown in. Inoculating the soil helps ensure the beneficial fungi are present to form a symbiotic relationship. For those who aren't aware, mycorrhizae are beneficial fungi that form special bonds with the roots of plants. They can act as an extension of the plant's own root system and helps absorb more water and nutrients from the soil. Plants that have established mycorrhizae relationships have been shown to be more drought tolerant and less susceptible to root diseases. Mycorrhizae have also been documented to share nutrients across plants of different species growing near each other.

- If your plant has developed more top growth than root growth, you can reduce transplant stress by pruning back the top growth. This becomes more important if you need to prune the roots or they get damaged. Until the plant gets established, it will have less of an ability to take up enough water to support its current vegetation.

After planting your tree, unless it is dormant, you need to keep up a regular watering schedule for at least 2 weeks, with the first watering being at the time of planting.. After that, water during times of low rainfall for 1-2 years at which point the tree should be fairly established. Depending on the time of the year, how often to water those first 2 weeks will vary. In Spring or Fall I water new transplants every other day with two gallons of water. In Summer, if I choose to plant something, I water everyday the first week and then switch to every other day the second week and monitor the plant for heat stress, watering when needed. For Winter, I water deeply at the time of planting and that's all.

With that, your fig tree should be planted for success. However, if in-ground planting isn't your thing, growing figs in containers is a viable alternative. If fact, it can be more advantageous than growing in the ground depending on where you live.

Should You Grow Figs In Containers

Growing a fig (or rather any tree) in the ground means more roots, which can support more growth. In simple terms, the plants get bigger. Who wouldn't want a bigger tree with more fruit?

Well actually, a lot of people don't want a big tree or even a lot of fruit.

If you are contemplating whether you should grow in the ground or in a container, it's important to analyze these pros and cons.

Pros and Cons of Container Growing Figs

Pros

- Restricts root growth, preventing the fig from damaging foundations and piping.

- Allows the plant to be mobile. An important aspect when trying to grow figs in colder climates.

- Allows you to use carefully crafted potting mixes optimal for the plant's growth and fruiting.

- Can add an additional design element to the space. Containers for figs can be small or large. Temporary or permanent.

- Allows for multiple trees that would otherwise crowd the space.

- They also let fig cuttings grow with no competition before transplanting.

- Allows for better water control. Too much water can cause figs to split and/or dilute the sugar(flavor) of the fruit.

Cons

- Containers need soil/potting mix which can start to get expensive when planting larger sizes.

- Aesthetically pleasing containers are very expensive and cost more than the actual plant.

- Plants in pots dry out a lot faster and experience more stress from temperature extremes.

- Fertilization needs to be applied more often as it leeches from the soil or gets used up by the plant.

- Fig trees use up organic matter quickly, causing potting mixes composed of mainly organic material to reduce in volume. You can notice this when the plant has separated the mix from the sides of the container.

- I have found that ants really like plants in containers more than those in the ground. They can turn the entire container into an ant mound.

- It can be difficult to get worms into your plant container.

As you can see, growing in a container comes with many negatives as well as positives, but the value of the positives are hard to pass up in certain situations. If you want to grow figs in a colder climate, containers are mandatory for many varieties since they will need to be placed in a protected location during winter or kept small so the trees are easy to cover. If you have a small property or rent your space, containers are also the way to go. Not only do you not want to be liable for damages caused by roots, but trying to dig up a fig tree to take with you is a lot of trouble and not worth it. A potted fig will likely outgrow a large one that has been heavily damaged, when transplanted.

For cheap potting mix, I use half composted cow manure and half peat moss. This creates a slightly acidic mix that allows for some lime to be added for calcium. Due to the high organic composition, it also retains water extremely well but needs to be replenished each season. To make the mix more permanent, you will need to add sand, silt, or clay. These are the foundation of all true soils and provide structure along with the ability to hold on to nutrients.

Potting mixes may also be lacking in trace minerals so adding rock dust is more beneficial than with in-ground planting. Rock dust is literally ground up rocks used to add minerals to the soil. I mix a suggested rate of 2 Tbsp. per gallon of water and only apply it annually.

Ways To Keep Ants and Pests Off Of Your Figs

When growing figs you will undoubtedly discover you aren't the only one who likes the sugary fruit. Indeed, most pests you encounter will be after the fruit rather than the vegetation. Of all the potential pests, two of the most persistent are birds and ants.

Ants are the easier of the two to deal with. They typically cause two problems: building a nest in the root zone of the tree and eating the sugar that seeps out of fruit. Rather than turning to harmful insecticides, there are organic approaches for dealing with each issue. To stop ants from forming mounds near your trees or in pots, sprinkle food-grade diatomaceous earth around the area.

Diatomaceous earth, also known as D.E. and diatomite, is a dust high in silica that relies on a physical interaction to control pests in the garden. While fairly safe for humans, D.E. is very fatal for insects. The tiny molecules absorb the protective oils on the exoskeleton of insects, causing them to dry out in a few days after exposure. If an ant bed pops up, simply sprinkle a generous amount onto and around the mound, allowing a week for it to go barren.

Take caution not to spread diatomaceous earth irresponsibly. The physical action of the dust can affect desirable garden pals such as ladybugs. **Also, be certain to only use food-grade D.E.** Industrial diatomaceous earth is often treated with toxic chemicals and is also ineffective at pest control.

If ants are crawling up your fig tree but there are no mounds at the base, spreading diatomaceous earth isn't the most practical decision, and may prove time-consuming to keep applied. Instead, in this instance, you will want to place a barrier around the trunk of the tree or individual stems.

There's more than one way to accomplish this but the simplest method I've experienced is to wrap aluminum foil around the trunk and spread a layer of vaseline on it. Most ants will be deterred by the vaseline but those that aren't will get stuck. If you aren't keen on using a petroleum product luckily some knowledgeable people saw a need and developed more natural products. One of those products is named **Tanglefoot Insect Barrier**. Application is the same, but they also have a paper band to use instead of aluminum foil. For thin trees, flagging tape can also be used.

Now onto the more troublesome pest...birds.

Birds will make you cry as they wait patiently to steal the most ripe figs. They won't even eat the whole thing. No. Instead, they leave a remnant of the fruit so you can imagine what you have missed. Sure enough, birds are demons in disguise for avid fig growers.

There isn't much you can do to protect against birds beyond the standard bird netting but even this poses a problem if you decide to grow a fig to a decent size. In addition, besides aesthetics, bird netting might not be ideal since you will need to check it daily to make sure no birds have gotten tangled. This issue is less of a problem if you can tighten the netting but for a large tree, that's a good bit of work. Some people use individual, breathable bags to protect fruit, but who really wants to go through that trouble?

The only other remedy I can offer is to **choose a fig that has green fruit when ripe**. Birds are less likely to go after them, leaving more for you to enjoy. This can be a problem for people in colder regions since the Chicago Hardy fig has purple fruit. There are some other cold-hardy figs with green fruit, but none as hardy as the Chicago fig.

Unfortunately, figs do not ripen once picked, so harvesting early won't work.

Other than ants and birds, figs are relatively pest free compared to other fruit trees. Most other problems can usually be solved with a few applications of neem oil.

As you grow figs, you may encounter some diseases such as fig mosaic virus. Fig mosaic virus is a virus transmitted by mites that cause abnormal leaves and growth in fig trees. There is no cure for the virus, therefore it's important to maintain a miticide spraying regimen if you are worried for your trees. Weekly applications of neem oil is good protection, however there are also commercial grade options available. I don't recommend synthetic pesticides, especially for a fruit tree, but that is your decision. If you think a tree has mosaic virus, it is recommended to discard the plant material that falls to the ground. If you keep the tree, always sterilize your pruners between each cut. Mosaic virus can be maintained by giving the fig tree great growing conditions, nutrients, and optimal water at all times. The virus is so common in some places that they don't even try to prevent it.

How and When To Prune A Fig Tree

Pruning a fig offers many benefits including better air circulation, desired growth habit, and optimal fruit production. Fig pruning should mainly be done in late Winter when the plant is dormant, unless it involves damaged, diseased, or dead tissue. Suckers/watersprouts should also be pruned at any time they appear if you don't plan on keeping them for fruit, since they can grow vigorously.

It takes around 3 years to prune a fig into a good structure.

I recommend only to top prune your tree after it has been established and grown to the height you desire. Normally, topping off trees is taboo for good reason, but for some fruiting plants it has merit. While waiting for your tree to grow, maintenance pruning just involves removing unhealthy limbs, overlapping limbs, and limbs growing inward. You also need to identify the stems you want to keep for fruiting and eliminate any others at the base to prevent crowding.

Figs fruit on new wood and possibly 1-year old wood, called a breba crop. That means, as the tree gets larger vertically, the fruit will become harder to reach. This is why the majority of figs you see are pruned to keep them as large shrubs or small trees. Old growth on figs have little value, fruit-wise and make harvesting more difficult. Large plants also become susceptible to wind and snow damage that causes limbs to break.

Once your tree has reached the desired height, cut back the terminal buds on all branches. This will cause additional branching in upcoming growth. More new branches, means more fruit for the main crop.

After this, maintenance pruning consists of the previous practices with the addition of cutting off all of the new growth from the previous season. Essentially, the goal is to have a base consisting of old wood for structure and keep encouraging new growth. If you have a fig that produces a breba crop on 1-year-old wood, you may want to switch to pruning every two years instead of one. This will create an alternation of some years with both a breba and main crop, and some years with just a main crop.

Open Center Pruning

While the above pruning method is my preferred, the open center pruning is also widely used. Open center revolves around getting the tree to grow as a single stem and then topping off the single stem once it reaches around knee or waist high. This will cause branching in a U-shape that keeps the center exposed to wind and sunlight, reducing disease issues, increasing fruit ripening, and allowing more space for fruiting branches to put out new growth.

Once the single stem is topped off, you want to proceed the same way as the first pruning method I discussed. Despite the benefits of an open center, I personally don't like the style because of the aesthetics. I like the charm of a lush multi-trunk shrub rather than the sparse tree-like appearance this method creates.

Rejuvenation Pruning

Rejuvenation pruning is for those who prefer to take a laid back approach to fig growing or are growing figs as herbaceous perennials. This method of pruning requires letting the fig grow naturally, producing several stems from the base. Once the plant has reached a height that isn't optimal you cut back one-third of the old branches annually, down to six inches or lower. By the third year, you will have a rejuvenated tree with high-performing growth.

Alternatively, you can also cut back all of the growth at once, but it will take a lot of energy from the tree to regrow. This heavy energy expenditure will affect the harvest for the current season but the tree should fully recover the following year.

Rejuvenation pruning is often necessary in areas where figs experience Winter damage. Winter desiccation can affect the entire top growth of the plant and must be pruned off. Many people find it easier to just reduce the entire plant down to 6 inches rather than trying to identify how damaged each branch is. This also allows the plant to grow uniformly.

A fig that requires rejuvenation pruning every year because of Winter damage is not ideal since it means you may never get an optimal crop.

Pinching Figs During Growing Season

While not exactly "pruning", you may also benefit from pinching the terminal bud of the new growth during the growing season. Because new growth will eventually be pruned back, pinching to stop the growth early and force fruiting is commonly performed. This technique is especially beneficial to those who live in zone 7 or lower, as the shorter season makes it more difficult to ripen figs.

Before pinching a branch you need to first make sure it has grown enough and developed a fig. To do this, check each stem node, between where the leaf attaches to the stem. There should be two dots. One is a bud and the other is a fig. If the two dots are present in at least one node, it is ok to pinch but you could wait for more if desired. If only one dot is there, it's not ready to be pinched.

Pinching isn't needed in warmer climates.

How To Take Fig Cuttings (get free plants)

With all of this talk about pruning figs, I want to discuss fig cuttings since the two go hand-in-hand. Every year, each pruning of your fig tree opens the possibility of creating new plants. Asexual propagation is the main way of producing new fig trees, with cuttings being the most popular method.

When pruning, any section that is thicker than a pencil and 6-8 inches in length will hold up well to propagation. You can even cut longer stems into smaller pieces.

Make an angled cut with sterilized pruners right below an axillary bud.

Depending on when you take a cutting, it can either be planted immediately or stored in the refrigerator.

Cuttings in late Winter/Early Spring can be planted immediately but cuttings in late Fall/Early Winter should be stored for future use.

To store a cutting, the use of an inorganic material is preferred. A lot of people will suggest storing in damp paper towels or newspaper but this often leads to mold issues. Rather, sterilize the cuttings with anti-microbial soap or a 10% bleach and water solution and allow it to dry. Once dried, dip the cut end into beeswax and allow it to harden. Wrap the cuttings in a form-fitting material, typically saran wrap. If saran wrap bothers you, you can experiment with beeswax saran wrap but I have not used it myself.

Once wrapped, store it in the fridge at around 40 degrees Fahrenheit. They should keep long enough to plant in early spring.

Most common fig cuttings aren't difficult to root and don't even need rooting hormone. Cutting the wax end back to the next node and sticking it in a moist potting mix is enough most times. Be sure to leave at least one bud above the soil.

Once planted it is imperative to make sure your fig cuttings do not dry out. I like to keep a clear reusable bag over my pots to create a mini-greenhouse effect. Take the bag off for a moment once a week and remove completely after the cutting has had roots for a month. Figs do not take long to root, but it is best to let them grow in place for a year before trying to transplant. You could also opt to place the cutting directly in the ground but this has lower odds of success than planting in a loose potting mix.

You can check to see if you cutting has roots by gently tugging at it. If you feel resistance, it should be rooted. Keep in mind that not even the best fig growers have a 100% success rate propagating new cuttings. It is best to do more than one cutting propagation to allow room for error. If the cutting refuses to root you can try peeling away the outer layer of bark, exposing the cambium tissue and dip in rooting hormone. However, I find these two steps excessive for figs.

Breba Crop vs Main Crop

You've seen me refer to breba and main crops several times already and may be wondering if it's an important consideration. Not every variety of fig produces a breba crop, which is on 1-year-old growth but every common fig does produce a main crop on new growth (some need pollination).

Depending on where you live, it is a good idea to analyze both. Because breba crops form before the tree goes dormant, it can be destroyed by harsh Winter or cold Spring weather but ripens earlier than the main crop. This makes them ideal for those with a short growing season. If you can't get a main crop, you can at least hope to get the breba crop.

If you live where there is no need for your breba crop, you can remove them to promote a better main crop. The size of the brebas can be larger compared to the mains but their taste is usually considered subpar. Brebas can also vary in color and shape compared to the mains. Some figs will also produce a breba crop that will ultimately drop off the tree before ripening.

Additionally, if you decide to grow figs for brebas rather than main crops, remember that it will change the pruning method. You will need to keep last season's growth to get a breba crop. Frost protection may also be required and fluctuating spring temperatures are undesirable.

Some fig varieties that have breba crops are: Marseilles (White), Nero 600m, Desert King, San Miro Piro, Kadota, Black Mission, LSU Gold and Brown Turkey.

Figs like Desert King, are often grown primarily for their breba crop because the main crop requires pollination by a fig wasp.

If you have a fig whose main crop isn't going to ripen, you can see more success with your breba crop by removing the main crop as it forms.

Are There Wasps Inside Of Figs?

You may have heard this or seen it in the comments of any popular fig video. "Fig have dead wasps in them, omg!"

Tell people to take a chill pill.

Every fig grower cringes at such irresponsible information. Understanding fig biology helps explain the basis for this exaggerated claim (not exactly false, but not exactly true). Figs are a special fruit being that they aren't really a fruit. What we call a fruit is actually a syconium. Syconium are basically flowers contained in fleshy sacks. As one can expect, flowers need to be pollinated to produce fruit in most circumstances.

Figs have developed a special relationship with a family of wasps, commonly referred to as fig wasps, taxonomically named *Agaonidae*. The female wasps transfer pollen from male figs (Capri figs) to edible female figs by entering through the hole at the fig apex, called an ostiole or "eye". The female wasps are searching for a place to lay eggs but a fig is not suitable for them, however, once they enter the fruit the wings are damaged and they cannot escape. They end up pollinating fruit and get dissolved by special enzymes the fig produces. The wasp becomes plant food. Crunchiness in figs are usually seeds or seed husks, NOT wasp parts or eggs.

There are 4 types of figs involved in this relationship: Capri figs, San Pedro figs, Smyrna figs, and Common figs. They can either be uniferous or biferous. Uniferous figs produce only one crop and biferous produce two.

Capri figs - are figs known to develop male flowers that provide the pollen needed to pollinate San Pedro and Smyrna figs. They can sometimes produce their own edible fruit but are mainly used for pollination purposes.

San Pedro figs - are a group of figs that produces a breba crop which doesn't need pollination and a main crop that will need pollination. Remember the Desert King example. *Be aware that there is also a fig plant identified as San Pedro. It also goes by the name, "Black Spanish."

Smyrna figs - produce only one crop that will need pollination by a fig wasp.

Common figs - refers to figs that will produce a crop with no pollination but that doesn't necessarily mean a wasp has not entered one. Note that the common fig-type is different from the common fig name. For example, Desert King is still a *Ficus carica* variety. People have the misconception that common figs are self-fertile but they are actually parthenocarpic, meaning they will produce fruit without pollination.

Despite the wasp being dissolved, this isn't to say a fig won't have an insect inside of it. How much the ostiole of figs opens up is another important consideration for fig growers.

Open-Eye vs Closed-Eye Figs

The "eye" of a fig refers to the petiole on the bottom of the fruit. Depending on the variety it can be open or closed. This specialized opening is why fig wasps are so important since other pollinators can't fit. However, many pests can. While the width of the eye is helpful in determining if it is open or closed, the final determination relies on the opening and it's ability to allow insects into the center of the fruit. Some small, open eyes look closed but can actually be open.

There are no real benefits to having an open-eye fig. Rather, it becomes a trait that restricts where a fig can be easily grown. The open eye acts as a pathway for water and pests to enter a fig and spoil it from the inside. Areas with humid environments and heavy rainfall can find it difficult to manage figs of this type. Not only do they spoil faster, but they are also more prone to splitting from overwatering.

If you do seek to grow an open-eye fig in a wet environment, it is best to choose a variety with a long neck. The neck, or peduncle, is the portion of the fruit between the stem and the fig. A long neck causes the fruit to drupe which helps protect from water getting in.

Pests will still be a bigger issue. Ants, in particular, love open-eye figs. You will likely need to implement the pest prevention I discussed previously and also take care to break open figs before consuming them to inspect the interior.

Some open-eyed varieties also release honey or resin that acts as a natural barrier to water. Figs that produce honey at the eye work for drier environments but it can get washed away from strong rain. Resin producing, open-eyed figs are more resistant to water and rain events.

Closed-eyed figs are less susceptible to pests and splitting making them the ideal choice. Ants may not even be an issue with closed figs.

How To Winterize Your Fig Tree

Winterizing your fig tree means to prepare it for cold weather, lessening the damage it sustains till Spring. Any zone lower than 8 should consider winterizing their fig or at least be prepared to protect it on the coldest nights. Remember that even if the tree itself does not get injured from the cold, the breba crop can be affected. For some colder areas, the breba crop is usually all you can rely on for a harvest.

Potted trees are easier to handle for Winter. In Fall, when the tree has gone dormant, you will want to prepare a space for them to stay until at least a week past your late frost date. Typically, an unheated garage or shed is a good environment. Some people use greenhouses but they can sometimes get warm enough to cause the plant to break dormancy early. If your potted fig tree has gotten too big to fit anywhere, it might be necessary to prune some limbs to make it more compact.

Potted fig trees should be placed in storage with damp soil. They shouldn't need irrigation, but if your soil does somehow dry, you will need to water it. Also note that there are several more ways to overwinter a potted plant but they aren't practical for the size of fig trees. Two of these methods include burying the pot in the ground and creating a layer of insulating organic material using metal mesh.

Winterizing an in-ground fig tree is where the real trouble begins. I highly don't recommend growing a fig tree in the ground if you need to prepare it for Winter. The process can require a lot of resources. The colder your area, the more thorough you will need to be. Additionally, if you want to protect the tree's breba crop (one-year-old wood), this becomes a necessity since you can't rely on the plant regrowing from the roots.

In-ground fig trees need to be insulated enough to protect against cold winds while also retaining heat built up during the day from the sun. I find the most effective way of achieving this is to wrap the tree in several layers of material. To do this you will need:

- Durable twine
- Burlap
- Painter cloth
- Bubble wrap
- Black tarp or plastic.
- Tape
- Leaf litter

This method of overwintering requires your fig tree to have fairly flexible stems. To begin, you need to bundle your stems together and tie them in a tepee fashion. Once tied together, you need to wrap a layer of burlap around the tree, followed by the painter cloth, then bubble wrap, and finish with the black tarp. Tie and secure with tape as you go. Once the tree is secured, place a generous layer of leaves around the base to add additional protection from cold wind. In the end you should be left with a tepee structure that has an opening at the top. That opening is your vent. Cover that opening with a bag or bucket that can be removed when needed. On very warm days it may be necessary to open the vent and let the hot air escape.

As you can see, this is a lot of material and effort that quickly builds up if you have several trees to overwinter. This is why I recommend growing figs in pots for cooler climates, despite the drawbacks it has or choose very cold-hardy varieties.

As stated before, wait at least a week after the last frost date and check the week-long forecast. If you are clear of cold weather it should be safe to remove all of the protection. Hopefully your figs have not sustained any damage and you can look forward to a successful crop for the season.

If you have a mature fig tree but temperatures are predicted to get abnormally cold, trying to wrap it might prove to be nearly impossible. Second-year wood or older is not very flexible. In such a case, the fig will likely be fine if the low temperature is not sustained for more than a few days. Still, if you want some assurance you can place incandescent christmas lights around the tree. Incandescent lights, unlike led lights, give off heat. It is usually enough to stop frost damage from occurring. This same option can be utilized if you happen to get a frost past the last frost date. Christmas lights should be viewed as quick, emergency protection and not relied on as the sole method of overwintering. While they do well to protect top growth, the plant roots could still get damaged if exposed to long periods of cold with no insulation.

List Of Common Fig Varieties

These are some of the most popular common fig varieties in North America. Some are easily accessible from nurseries but others may need to be acquired by a fellow fig grower. When getting figs, if you are purchasing, only buy from certified sellers with a good reputation. The selling of fake fig varieties is a surprisingly large practice on online marketplaces. Sometimes, even if someone didn't mean to sell a fake variety, the confusion can come from the way figs are mainly referred to by their common names. Common names can overlap and several varieties can have the same name with very little physical differences. Often times you can't tell what kind of fig you have until the fruit has formed.

Popular Varieties

Alma - Cold-hardy fig that has unique, brownish yellow fruit. The figs ripen and develop spots similar to a banana. Known to be very sweet. Open-eye but produces a resin.. Uniferous.

Black Mission - Also known as San Pedro (yes, very confusing). A favorite of the south. Produces an aesthetically desirable fruit with a rich, purple skin and red pulp. Very productive and starts fruiting earlier than most other figs. Very small, open eye. Biferous.

Brown Turkey (Southeastern) - Very popular fig in the southeast for is relative cold hardiness. Vigorous grower in warm areas but can experience heavy Winter damage when young. Small to medium, purple fruit. Has a small, open eye. Biferous.

Celeste - Another fig favored in the Southeast for its cold tolerance but may still require Winter protection. Less vigorous than Brown Turkey with small to medium, brownish fruit. Considered very sweet, hence its other name, sugar fig. Closed-eye variety. Considered uniferous but some reports established trees of producing brebas but it's not to be expected.

Chicago Hardy - Popular fig for Eastern states. Exceptional cold hardiness. Grows well once established but not the most vigorous. Produces a reliable abundance of small, purple fruit. Sweet taste but not very unique. Biferous, but not a heavy breba producer. Closed eye.

Conadria - An early fruiting fig that produces large, green fruit. Valued for its less vigorous growth and prolific fruiting, making it ideal for container growing. Very small, open eye. Biferous.

Desert King - One of the best San Pedro figs for breba production. Has good cold tolerance, making it a possible fig for those living in the East to Southeast. Extremely productive producing very large, green fruit. Taste has been known to vary from being very sweet to bland. Open-eye that is prone to splitting.

Italian 258 - A popular fig among enthusiasts. The I-258 is known to be highly productive and vigorous once rooted. Produces medium-sized, purple fruit with a large eye. Prized for its complex flavor among figs. Biferous.

Italian Honey - As the name suggests, has a sickly sweet flavor. Produces a yellow-green fruit with a closed eyed. One of the more drought-tolerant figs, producing better tasting fruit with less watering.

Kadota - The fig used in fig newton bars, this variety is slightly cold-hardy and productive, but prefers having some Winter protection. Has a vibrant, green fruit with an open eye that produces honey. Fruit size is small to medium. Can produce a high-quality breba crop. Biferous.

LSU Gold - Large, yellow fig developed by Louisiana State University fig breeding program. Very sweet, distinctive fig flavor. Large open eye but secretes honey to seal. Very susceptible to splitting and spoiling in rainy areas. Biferous.

LSU Purple - Smaller than the LSU Gold. Another result from Louisiana State University breeding program. Closed-eye making it better suited for wetter areas than Gold. Biferous, but breba crop is reported to be unreliable.

Olympian Hardy - another cold-hardy variety that produces reliable crops. Breba crop is also well adapted to cold weather, still producing in Spring even after Winter lows into the teens. Has medium-sized, purple fruit with a closed eye. Biferous.

Panache Tiger Stripe - Considered one of the most beautiful fig fruits, featuring green and yellow stripes with red pulp. New bark also has very faint stripes. Known to ripen late so needs a long growing season. Strawberry-like flavor. Open eye. Uniferous.

Ronde de Bordeaux - Another early fruiting fig for those with a short season. Cold-hardy and able to regrow vigorously from the roots after Winter. Reliable, moderate producer of small to medium-sized, purple fruit. Closed eye. Biferous in areas where it does not die back to the ground.

Violette de bordeaux - Very fragrant fig with stunning, black-purple fruit and red pulp. Considered a top tasting fig by many experts. A very cold-hardy fig and reliable producer but not very vigorous. Closed eye. Biferous.

This list of figs is far from being all-inclusive. As you continue your fig adventure, you will discover that there are an endless supply of varieties. Each has their own unique properties and taste. Remember that the quality of figs and their performance can vary widely depending on where they are grown. Something that is a top-tasting and producing fig in California may not do well in Florida. Despite warm temperatures other variables such as rain, humidity, and soil can influence the health of the plant and fruit quality.

Hopefully, this book has inspired you to go out and get your first fig plant or more. Sure enough, like many people, once you get started it will be difficult to stop collecting new varieties.

Thank you for reading!

Printed in Great Britain
by Amazon